I0755977

FINISHING LINE PRESS
www.finishinglinepress.com

UNFINISHED SPACES

poems by

Susan Hunter

Finishing Line Press
Georgetown, Kentucky

UNFINISHED SPACES

ISBN 979-8-88838-439-8 First Edition

ACKNOWLEDGMENTS

Many thanks to the editors of the following publications where some of these poems, or earlier versions, have previously appeared:

Southern Humanities Review: "Door"
Saranac Review: "Father"
Poem: "Leaving"
The Chaffin Journal: "On Viewing Childe Hassam"; "The Girls' Rooms"
Illya's Honey: "Gone"

Publisher: Leah Huete de Maines
Editor: Christen Kincaid
Cover Art: Julie Grooms
Author Photo: Arnie Weiss
Cover Design: Elizabeth Maines McCleavy

Order online: www.finishinglinepress.com
also available on amazon.com

Author inquiries and mail orders:
Finishing Line Press
PO Box 1626
Georgetown, Kentucky 40324
USA

Contents

To Bill

To you, I bequeath . . .

I'll take them all with me in sacks.
Fantasies, bad dreams,
cars heading nowhere,
lost grocery bags,
lost grandchildren,
those who wouldn't listen,
illnesses that won't quit.

Or, I'll leave them all behind,
a momentous irresponsibility.
I'm done with all this,
and you can do what you want with it.

It will be stacked on a bookshelf
next to my moldy diplomas,
picture of my great grandmother,
poster I bought when I danced
in a sheared beaver coat.
All the stuff.
For you to decide.

I'm taking my life with me,
stronger than ever,
still burning with whatever
keeps my imperfect heart going.

I'm leaving a Korean mother-of-pearl box,
a bookmark, a gold clock.

Just don't throw it all away.
I've written something
over the years, for you.

Astronomy

Red maple trees in fall,
morning sunlight on the porch
and Haydn's arias.

The woman scientist said
we should thank our lucky stars
to have lived at this time
of rushing mass propelled by
the big bang.

Our moon, faithful disc,
keeps us both tethered
and sane,
and a child I know asks
"Is heaven far away?"

Look out through the night,
past the sunset striped by heat.
Hold onto my hand
as we spend one last day on the beach,
waves going out, coming in,
out and in.

You throw stones into the water,
and off the cliff, searching for a fin
past the salt-and-pepper sand.

I peer at Comet Neowise
whose filmy fish tail
squirms through Ursa Major.

Keep my universe close . . .
sun brightening wildflowers,
a seashell in a small hand,
mist painting hills on the river's far bank.

Macbeth

The hearts
strung out on metal wire.
From heart to heart.
You broke mine.
I sat on a stone step.
You sewed others together.

Mine broke again,
and another man sewed it together.
Then his heart broke, and I offered words
to close wounds caused by another man
who broke hearts and bodies apart in
another part of the world.

Not just separated by distance,
But by long stretches of time
over a long clothesline,
when a man and a woman in a play set
in the dark ages, performed dark deeds,
throwing young children into fire pits,
slitting throats while people slept.

Now, in this modern age,
a five-year-old is shot in the Ukraine,
and she dies and her body lies
under her little cloth coat.

Nantucket

is the place
I went with you.
I'm a girl with brown hair pulled back,
lying in a field of daisies, holding one.

I was smiling at you who just said
"I wouldn't care if I never saw your mother again."

On the bicycle, I looked back
at your large, pale face.
Not many smiles.
I didn't bring them out.
And on the ferry, you looked at a child rubbing its eyes.
"The baby is tired," you said.

I loved you.
But too many jagged edges
of the very young
didn't fit together,
unthought-out words,
casual in their catastrophe.

Still, it was a perfect island,
shimmering harbor, meadows of grass.
I remember the foghorn
moaning out into the night ocean
as a metronome clocking all the sadness of shipwrecks,
of wives on widows' walks,
of those lost, who never came back.

At the bird feeder

I think it's the birds I will miss most.
When you think of their feathers,
bright yellow against black, white against gray.

I hear their songs when early spring
crawls across the soil.
So hopeful, those three notes,
the invisible bird
hides in unblossomed branches.

I recall the robin's song that is my childhood,
the upright wet grass balancing
a cracked bird's egg.

My daughter thinks a cardinal is my mother,
And I could believe them ethereal.
But with us, they wait and wait for warm weather,
wait for sunlight to warm the sand.

Today, when we walk the beach,
a gull moves head-on toward us,
daring and cock-sure.
Those sandpipers, as if tied together,
shift as one body through the mirror wave.

I think about the birds
springing off the ground
and flying over everything we live in—
the almost perfect harbor and the thread
of a road tied taut to a knob of land
in the middle of the bay.

I thought about praying to a cardinal
when I was sick,
cynical eyes open,
and feeling better soon.

I gave my mother's cardinal painting
to my daughter.
It watches over her house,
waiting for spring.

Father

Outside, through the window,
the frozen pond
is blistering in the January sun.

Here, in the room where my father dies,
the curtains are drawn dark
to shield the world from a life
that has been reduced to gasps.

Amid breathlessness,
the ancient civilizations he studied
don't amount to a hill of beans.

As I glance above his head,
mourning the loss of conversation,
laughter and sweet pipe smoke,
a halo spreads from wall to wall.
Blocks of light, build to a miraculous
shining thing his eyes can't see.

The vision fades too quickly to call witness,
leaving a razor-thin thread of hope
to see him looking once more at me
from the empty holy corner.

Dreams of my father

In my dream, the summer I went to Korea,
my father was lost,
less than Buddha,
the bronzed god
smiling, fingers in yoga mudra
embracing all,
from the lowest,
who dodged through the narrow street,
clutching a greasy mandu,
to the highest temple monk
who felt the mountain breeze waft through
the wet, heat-charged air.
In child's pose,
knees aching,
he bowed toward the giant, smiling statue.

In my dream, my father and I
went to church together.
The minister smiled.
And then, underground, I lost my father
who was dressed in the suit and tie he wore to
Korea that long ago summer

He took a plane with
propellers grinding
and greeted people sick of war.
They smiled, and gave him
The keys to open Seoul.

I was young then, just getting by,
hoping he would come home.
"How did you circle the earth alone?"
I should have asked.
Instead, I traveled to that land 50 years later
and dreamed
that he was lost

I needed to strike the gong stone
that rang out in the forest.
"My father is gone!"

When he reappeared,
He was a round Buddha-likeness,
sad, like a boy who had been searching
for the gifts he had brought to the temple,
sad, like the man who misplaced the mother of pearl
for the daughter he left behind.

Door

Door I'd come in and out
and in and out with lilacs in my hands,
angry over her, over him, over her and over him.

Door I came through after ice and snow.
Door she bolted to keep us out.
Door I ran out of to do what I loved.

Door my daughter slammed.
Door the ghost came through
with house-warming embrace.

Door closed after I had left.
Sound of shutting,
of breaking heart apart.

The girls' rooms

They're empty of girls now,
and what stays are the smiles
of those you knew
pasted in collages stuck to the walls.

Pets' ashes lie in small boxes,
and stuffed animals bask in sunlight
that pours through lacy curtains not heavy
enough to keep out the cold.

The clothes that didn't go with them hang
in all the dusty rooms that dot the seacoast
where guests sleep, glancing at
biology papers and bunches of fake flowers.

A guitar sits in one corner; a flute is smothered in a bureau drawer.
You crank open the window, let in fresh air,
and close the door.
In the corner, a doll sits on a chair
with tears in her eyes.

Gone

In my dream, ticking like a metronome,
I climb the hill to your stone
that's straight and new, like a soldier with
no more stories to tell.
Rain pelts the tooth picked rise and marsh,
and I bring a yellow rose.

Someday, when they get around to it,
they'll inscribe your name
on the roster of spirits
that rise and fall on this hillside.

Someday, a pony-tailed girl
will work on a grave rubbing
and hang it on her wall.

I think how you guided me around your city
before we shared the wine,
and you spoke fluent Spanish to the waiter.
In my dream, you and I sit at either end
of a long, candlelit table.
If memory serves me, you handed me a flower
on a dusky summer evening.

Now, I must hurry away.
The clouds fill and spit
on the cold lake water.
One sweep over the stone,
and I'm gone to find my own slumber.

Unfinished spaces

You return often to that house,
walking through the front door,
down the large hall clouded with your father's pipe smoke.
As you head up the stairs,
the mouse circles your mother's feet again.
She laughs as you play the piano in the living room
and chase notes as they run away.

In your grandparents' house,
you spill the jewelry box onto the bedcovers,
while the dancing ballerina does a pirouette
to a hurdy-gurdy sound.

The room where you found your life again
was stripped bare that last night.
You tried to put it back together
forcing stubborn puzzle pieces into a headache.
One day, you'll remember it as it was
on sunny mornings, your young daughter close by,
the woodpecker tapping on the wall,
the white birch scraping its branches across the wood.

Grandson

Holding you there on my lap,
in the rocking chair,
in your room that was your room
before you were born,
I want to remember the moment
your eyes turned to the crib
where you usually lie.

Did you see them smiling there,
the ones I can't see anymore,
the ones I never knew?
Or did you begin waking up to
where you are,
where you were
and where you'll be?

I remember myself in adolescent fury
and my grandmother saying,
"You were such a sweet little girl!"

Will I say that also to you?
That you were a sweet little boy
and that I remember
the moment I held you on my lap
in the rocking chair,
in the room that was yours
before you were born?

Leaving

The last times go unrecognized.
How dense, fog-draped we are
at candlelit dinner tables,
on porches with rocking chairs
facing the ocean.

A tennis ball streaks over the net,
and a thousand nights pass unnoticed
before you all leave.

No warning when you go,
that it will be forever,
that there will be silence
as deep and dark as unmoving pines.

How do we not fret as you leave us
to shelter our children?
We have no preparation for what is
etched into shadows, the sagging skin,
hieroglyphics on the tomb.

Thankful

If memory is fickle,
I didn't travel to a small, zinc-smelting town
elbowed to the side of Blue Mountain
on Thanksgiving.
My aunt, denizen of her Pennsylvania hamlet,
arose at 5 a.m. to start cooking.
Turkey melting off its large bones, chestnut stuffing,
potato stuffing, green beans and cranberries,
shoo fly pie and cupcakes, corn and relish salad.

Later, Queenie would stop by
and draw portraits of my brother and me,
her gnarled hands gripping the pencil.
She and her car, my aunt later said,
were hit on the tracks by the 5:13 train
leaving Chicago.
Her portraits of little kids,
barrette in hair, bow tie, were stuffed
in a basement box on subterranean journeys
from one damp New England house to another.

If memory is fickle—or made up—
Pilgrim children dressed in top hats and buckles
didn't sit at a long table with Indians
enjoying turkey and cranberries.
The feast lasted three days, they say, and all sat
on the ground near the large bay,
thankful for those still alive,
before their grandchildren headed west.

Seville Sunday

The call of the dove fills space
between church bell chime and trellis
climbing up the walls of our tiny patio.
Only a square of sky blue sends down the hottest air.

In triple coo, the bird asks,
"Where have you gone?
Where are you going?
Where are you?"

In more frantic tremolo, its call echoes down the years, the centuries
through the gardens of the Alcazar and the warm fountains,
making a beeline to the Azores and across the ocean in mist,
time-traveler.
It re-sounds in my grandmother's dining room.
"Listen!" she said to me.
"It's the mourning dove."

It was the owl hooting in the woods
to the little girl lost and far from home.

Or that Eurasian dove call
moving across the snow tops east of the Alhambra
to fall on the cupped ears
thirsty and far below.

Cape Cod Bay

There are unhappy spirits here . . .
Wives overboard, dead babies,
Indians caught in the claws of plague
and those too weak to bury them.

Heads on spikes, skulls in sand dunes,
death in the planting fields.

Have the spirits left the beaches,
the rough surf,
a million sun flecks on Cape Cod Bay?
Now come the tourists to Plymouth Rock,
to the Italianate tower at Provincetown,
white man's stones piled to mark the landing,

The Mayflower's women washed clothing
In freshwater ponds on their first trip off the ship.
How the water must have tasted to drink!
How the sun shone, teasing the visitors,
settling in to killing cold.

The wind still whispers through these inland pines . . .
wives overboard, dead babies,
Indians caught in the claws of plague.
We gape at a tooth hidden
beneath a single maple leaf.

Caribbean sunrise

The first time I heard the sun rise,
it woke me from sleep in Guadeloupe.
It was a sound like a wind blowing,
and the birds were caught up in it,
and the sky brightened to white light.

In Simpson Bay, I watched as
the sun toiled up behind the hills,
and the trade winds
blew in from the east,
nudging the goldenness.

The doves woke,
and the fireball lit up
the back of the cloudbank to bright pink
that drained away
to a white-heated day.

Northward, the sun rises over the Potomac
as the river widens into the sea
off the Maryland shore.

Sun with the sound of
all our days,
the wake of the fisherman's boat
catches its early light.
Its dusky pink
lightens the river,
taking a prism path to that southern sea
where I first heard the sunrise,
brightening the sky to white light,
waking the doves beyond the cloudbank.

Tucson

I sit
on a shining
hardwood floor
and look out
at a 6 a.m. gray sky.

All night, the wind whips
in and out of the room.
A train whistle cries
across the desert,
and because it's unknown land,
it could be a train
going from nowhere
to nowhere.

Lonely is a house
sitting on a patch
of southwest sand.
Lonely is a sunset of red,
pink and gold
with a strip of blue.

Emily Dickinson

closed doors,
slammed them,
turned the lock.
She kept inside,
as she opened words
like doors,
sliced them open,
like tin cans
splashing out pain of a meadow
aching with dandelions.

Words in slanted scrawl
like skeins of wool
hidden in shut desk drawers,
scratched out on scraps,
on gilded stationery.

Emily Dickinson died
after crafting
an eternity of deaths,
syllables whirling
in eddies
like needles poking through
her unlived centuries.

I search for that phrase
pulled back through the eye
to a green, grassy space,
a candle in a midnight room.

On viewing Childe Hassam

We all looked at the beautiful pictures
painted in a time before we were born,
in a century before the last one,
before the horrors of just yesterday
and the day before.
And we drank in the colors of the roses
whose petals had fallen on the table.

A woman looked into a mirror beside an open window.
The sunlight poured into the room filled with daffodils.
It was morning, and a younger woman was reading on a settee.
She was wearing a dress and stockings.
Why not?
It was a beautiful world, this world of the painting.
It was the world that preceded our childhoods or the childhoods we never had.

In the painting where the sun didn't shine,
there was the shimmering of wet city pavement.
Mothers took children by the hand
and led them to a warm and comfortable place.
The city had a clear view of blue sky
down to the harbor.

In the world of the heart, when a grassy lawn leads up to a clapboard house,
it means the ocean is a stone's throw away.
Lunch is almost ready, and the aroma of lilies and lilacs
overwhelms the senses.
We don't need to strain the ear to make out the music.
A woman in lace plays the piano, while her sister sits nearby.
Softly, close the door so as not to disturb the slow cadence
of the passing years.

Susan Hunter's poems have appeared in *Southern Humanities Review, Saranac Review, The Chaffin Journal, Poem* and *Illya's Honey*. She was a contest winner in the Plymouth (MA) Poetry contest in 2020 and attended the Bread Loaf Writer's Conference in 2017 as a general contributor in poetry. She has read her poetry in venues in Connecticut and Massachusetts as well as on Cape Cod NPR radio and local arts television shows in Plymouth, MA where she lives with her husband. She has made her living as a newspaper editor and freelance journalist.

www.ingramcontent.com/pod-product-compliance
Lightning Source LLC
LaVergne TN
LVHW090542110826
845146LV00003B/1231

* 9 7 9 8 8 8 8 3 8 4 3 9 8 *